THE CASE of the Lost WORLD HERITAGE

You will know the truth and the truth will set you free.

Art: Mychailo Kazybrid

Script: Ed Chatelier

Lettering and Color and Cover Design: Richard Thomas

Creative Concept: EDGE GROUP Creative Media Agency

contact: edgesword@yahoo.com

+447905960775

THANKS TO:

Vesna Vujicic-Lugassy UNESCO, Gina Doubleday UNESCO

Michiko Tanaka UNESCO, Ian Denison UNESCO

Thanks to UNESCO.

First published in Great Britain in 2016

by Edge Group,
138 Grove Hall Court
London, NW8, UK

Copyright © UNESCO and Edge G3 Limited, 2016

DISCLAIMER

The designations employed and the presentations of material throughout this publication do not imply the expression of any opinion whatsoever on the part of UNESCO concerning the legal status of any country, territory, city or area or of its authorities, or concerning the delimitation of it's frontiers or boundaries.

The ideas and opinions expressed in this publication are those of the authors; they are not necessarily of UNESCO and do not commit the Organisation.

ISBN:

97809569731-7-7

MANKIND'S HERITAGE IS DISAPPEARING BEFORE OUR VERY EYES

HERITAGE SITES BELONG TO THE WORLD

WORLD HERITAGE IS MEANT TO BE ENJOYED BUT ALSO TO EDUCATE AND INSPIRE.

HERITAGE BELONGS TO ALL HUMANKIND

NATIONS NEED TO PROTECT THEIR HERITAGE.

HERITAGE IS AN IRREPLACABLE ESSENTIAL TO LIFE

LOSS OF HERITAGE WILL HURT FUTURE GENERATIONS.

UNESCO IS THE OIL THAT MAKES THE WORLD HERITAGE WORK SMOOTHLY. THE GLUE THAT KEEPS IT TOGETHER.

PATRIMONITO MEANS SMALL HERITAGE AND REPRESENTS THE YOUNG HERIATGE GUARDIAN.

CLIMATE CHANGE IS AFFECTING NATURAL HERITAGE SITES

HERITAGE IS A LEGACY FOR FUTURE GENERATIONS.

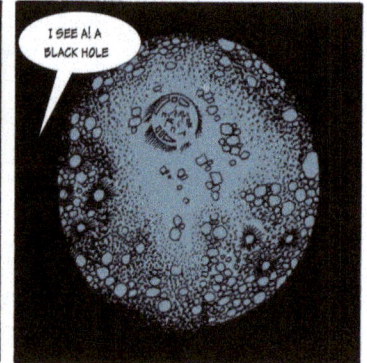

HERITAGE SITES MUST BE TREATED WITH RESPECT.

HERITAGE CAN HIGHLIGHT EPISODES IN HISTORY THAT SHOULD NOT BE REPEATED.

www.ingramcontent.com/pod-product-compliance
Lightning Source LLC
Chambersburg PA
CBHW061123010526
44112CB00025B/2955